Merry Christmas From Texas

by

Katherine Helms

McClanahan
Publishing House

International Standard Book Number 0-913383 66 X
Library of Congress Catalog Card Number 99 63303

Cover design and book layout by James Asher Graphics

Manufactured in the United States of America

All book order correspondence should be addressed to:

McClanahan Publishing House, Inc.
P.O. Box 100
Kuttawa, KY 42055
270-388-9388
1-800-544-6959
email: kybooks@apex.net
www.kybooks.com

To

Martha Cunningham Lewis

my mother, who taught me how to celebrate the season.

Merry Christmas from Texas

Christmas is a time to celebrate with family and friends; therefore, these recipes are easy to prepare, using everyday ingredients, and allow more time to enjoy the holiday season. Since Christmas is also a time of gift giving, I have included a special section on "gift giving goodies". These recipes are simple, yet provide special ways to show people that you care.

Merry Christmas from Texas reflects my effort to capture the unique tastes of Texas along with traditional fare. I wish to thank my good friends in Texas for contributing some of their favorite holiday recipes. I would also like to thank my family, especially my husband, Vance, for supporting me in this endeavor.

Merry Christmas to you!

Katherine Helms

Table of Contents

Appetizers 7
Beverages 23
Breads 37
Breakfast and Brunch 51
Soups and Salads 69
Side Items 87
Entrees 103
Desserts 127
Candies and Cookies 149
Gift Giving Goodies 165

Appetizers

Smokies in Two-Steppin' Sauce

One 9-ounce jar mustard
One 9-ounce jar grape jelly
16-ounces cocktail smokies

Mix together mustard and jelly. Place in a crock pot with smokies and allow to heat for 1 hour before serving. Serve with toothpicks. Serves 20.

Never Enough Cheese Bites

5 eggs
1 cup cottage cheese
¼ cup flour
½ teaspoon baking powder
¼ cup butter, melted
2 tablespoons minced green onions
One 4.5-ounce can green chiles, drained
2 cups shredded Monterey Jack cheese

Beat eggs and cottage cheese until smooth. Add flour, baking powder, and butter until well blended. Stir in green onions, chiles, and cheese. Pour into a greased 8-inch square pan. Bake at 350 degrees for 35 minutes. Cool slightly and cut into squares. Serves 25.

Southwest Sausage Squares

1 cup biscuit mix
⅓ cup milk
¼ cup mayonnaise
1 pound sausage
1 cup chopped onion
1 egg, beaten
2 cups shredded sharp cheddar cheese
Two 4.5-ounce cans green chiles, drained

Combine biscuit mix, milk, and 2 tablespoons mayonnaise; stir well. In a skillet, brown sausage and onion; drain. In another bowl, combine beaten egg, cheese, remaining mayonnaise, and chiles. Layer in a greased 9 x 13 baking dish: biscuit mix, sausage and onions, and then cheese mixture. Bake at 350 degrees for 30 minutes. Let stand 5 minutes before serving. Cut into squares. Serves 25.

Blazing Saddle Sausage Balls

1 pound sausage
1 egg, beaten
⅓ cup bread stuffing
½ cup catsup
1 tablespoon chili powder
1 tablespoon soy sauce
1 tablespoon vinegar
2 tablespoons brown sugar
½ cup water

Combine sausage, egg, and stuffing. Mix well and form into balls. Brown in skillet; drain. Add catsup, chili powder, soy sauce, vinegar, sugar, and water to the skillet. Return balls to skillet and simmer 30 minutes. Refrigerate or freeze. Reheat when ready to serve. Serves 30.

Popular Tortilla Pinwheels

8 ounces cream cheese, softened
One 4.5-ounce can chopped green chiles
¼ teaspoon garlic salt
2 tablespoons picante sauce
2 tablespoons chopped pecans
4 large flour tortillas

Mix together all ingredients except tortillas. Spread mixture on tortillas and roll like a jellyroll. Wrap in wax paper; refrigerate. Cut into ½-inch slices. Serves 10.

Holiday Ham Rolls

Two packages pre-baked dinner rolls in foil pan
8 ounces ham, thinly sliced
12 ounces Swiss cheese, sliced
½ cup butter, melted
1½ tablespoons poppy seed
1½ tablespoons prepared mustard
1½ tablespoons Worcestershire sauce
1 teaspoon onion flakes

Do not separate rolls. Slice top from rolls in one piece. Leaving bottoms in the foil pan, layer ham and cheese on rolls. Replace tops. Combine butter, poppy seed, mustard, Worcestershire sauce, and onion flakes; mix well. Drizzle over rolls. Refrigerate until butter is firm. Bake covered with foil at 350 degrees for 20 minutes. Cut into small pieces. Good served hot or cold. Serves 12.

Pineapple Cheese Ball

4 ounces cream cheese, softened
One 8-ounce can crushed pineapple, drained
¼ cup chopped green pepper
1 cup chopped pecans
2 tablespoons chopped onion
1 tablespoon garlic salt

Combine all ingredients in a bowl, saving 2 tablespoons chopped pecans. Mix well, shape into a ball and roll in reserved pecans. Chill for 2 hours. Serve with crackers. Serves 10.

Salado Spinach/Artichoke Dip

One 6-ounce jar spicy marinated artichoke hearts
5 ounces frozen spinach, shredded
One 10¾-ounce can cream of mushroom soup
½ cup grated Parmesan cheese
1 cup grated Monterey Jack cheese
½ cup mayonnaise
½ teaspoon salt
½ teaspoon garlic salt
1 tablespoon sour cream

Drain and chop artichoke hearts. Drain water from thawed spinach. Mix all ingredients except sour cream. Place in shallow baking dish and bake at 350 degrees for 15 minutes until bubbly and lightly browned. Garnish with sour cream. Serve with tortilla chips. Serves 20.

Colors of Christmas Artichoke Dip

One 6-ounce jar artichoke hearts
1 cup mayonnaise
One 2-ounce jar pimentos
One 4.5-ounce jar chopped green chiles
1 cup Parmesan cheese
½ teaspoon garlic salt

Drain and chop artichoke hearts. Mix all ingredients. Place in a greased 8 x 8 baking dish and bake at 350 degrees for 20 minutes. Serve hot with wheat crackers. Serves 20.

Guacamole Grande

2 avocados, mashed
½ pint sour cream
1 tablespoon picante sauce, medium or hot
1½ cups shredded Monterey Jack cheese
½ cup chopped green onions

Arrange in layers: avocados, sour cream, picante sauce, cheese, and green onions. Serve with tortilla chips. Serves 10.

TexMex Layered Dip

3 medium avocados, mashed
2 tablespoons lemon juice
½ teaspoon salt
¼ teaspoon pepper
1 cup sour cream
½ cup mayonnaise
1 package taco seasoning
Two 10½-ounce cans bean dip
1 cup chopped green onions
3 medium tomatoes, chopped
1 cup chopped black olives
1 cup shredded cheddar cheese

Mix avocado, lemon juice, salt, and pepper. In a separate bowl mix sour cream, mayonnaise and taco seasoning. In large pan layer: bean dip, avocado mixture, and sour cream mixture. Top with onions, tomatoes, olives, and cheese. Serve with tortilla chips. Serves 20.

Chili Con Queso Dip

3 tablespoons finely chopped onion
1 clove garlic, pressed
½ tablespoon butter
One 4.5-ounce can chopped green chiles
2 cups processed cheese spread
1 cup cheddar cheese
7 tablespoons evaporated milk

Sauté onion and garlic in butter until transparent. Add chiles and cheeses. Heat on low until cheese melts. Blend in evaporated milk. Serve with tortilla chips.

Special Occasion Spread

8 ounces canned kidney beans, drained
1 clove garlic, pressed
¼ teaspoon hot pepper sauce
1 teaspoon mayonnaise
2 tablespoons fresh lemon juice
½ teaspoon minced chives

Mix together all ingredients except chives. Blend until smooth, about 1 minute. Turn into serving bowl and sprinkle with chives. Serve with raw vegetables or crackers. Makes about 1 cup.

Fabulous Fruit Dip

8 ounces lemon yogurt
8 ounces sour cream
1 teaspoon ginger
½ teaspoon cinnamon
1 tablespoon honey
½ teaspoon grated lemon peel
½ teaspoon lemon juice

Combine all ingredients. Blend well. Cover and refrigerate 1 to 2 hours. Serve with assorted fresh fruits. Makes about 2 cups.

Beverages

Home for the Holidays Hot Chocolate

4 ounces unsweetened chocolate
¼ cup water
4 cups milk
½ cup half-and-half
½ cup sugar
¼ teaspoon salt
¼ teaspoon ground mace
1 teaspoon vanilla
½ teaspoon almond extract
½ cup whipped topping
⅛ teaspoon nutmeg

Combine chocolate and water in saucepan; stir over low heat until chocolate melts. Gradually add milk, half-and-half, sugar, salt, and mace. Cook over medium heat; stirring until mixture is hot. Stir in vanilla and almond flavoring. Pour into cups and garnish with whipped topping and nutmeg. Makes 5 cups.

Hostess' Favorite Hot Buttered Rum

1 pound butter, softened
1 pound light brown sugar
1 pound powdered sugar
2 teaspoons ground cinnamon
2 teaspoons ground nutmeg
1 quart vanilla ice cream, softened
Light rum or rum extract
Whipped cream
Cinnamon sticks

Combine butter, sugars, and spices; beat until light and fluffy. Add ice cream, stirring until well blended. Freeze. To serve, thaw slightly. Place 3 tablespoons mixture and 1 jigger (1 ounce) of rum or $\frac{1}{8}$ teaspoon of rum extract in a large mug; fill with boiling water. Stir well. Refreeze any unused mixture. Top with whipped cream and serve with cinnamon stick stirrers. Serves 25.

Cozy Christmas Eve Cocktail

3 cups pineapple juice
3 cups cranberry juice cocktail
½ cup packed brown sugar
1⅓ cups water
1 small cinnamon stick
1½ teaspoons whole clove

Combine juices, brown sugar and water in electric percolator; mix well. Break cinnamon stick into 3 pieces. Combine with cloves in basket of percolator. Run through per cycle. Serves 10.

Warm You Up Wassail

1½ cups sugar
4 cups boiling water
3 allspice berries
6 whole cloves
1 tablespoon ground ginger
One 1-inch stick cinnamon
1⅓ cups orange juice
⅔ cup lemon juice

Combine sugar and 2 cups boiling water; boil 5 minutes. Add spices, cover and allow to stand 1 hour. Add remaining water and fruit juices; mix well. Strain. Heat to boiling point. Serve immediately. Makes about 1 quart.

Easy Apple Cider

1 gallon apple juice
10 ounces red hots

Heat apple juice and red hots in a large pot until red hots are melted. Stir occasionally. Makes one gallon.

Angelic Almond Tea

4 cups water
1 cup sugar
¼ cup lemon juice
1½ cups hot tea
3 cups pineapple juice
¼ cup instant orange breakfast drink mix
1 teaspoon almond extract
1 teaspoon vanilla

Combine water, sugar, and lemon juice in saucepan; simmer 5 minutes. Add remaining ingredients; cook until thoroughly heated. Makes 2 quarts.

Buckle Down Boiled Custard

One 3¾-ounce package French vanilla instant pudding mix
¾ cup sugar
½ teaspoon vanilla
4 cups milk
One 8-ounce carton whipped topping

Add pudding mix, sugar and vanilla to milk. Stir until smooth. Fold in whipped topping. Chill until very cold. Serves 8.

Front Porch Tea

2 cups sugar
¾ cup powdered lemonade mix
½ cup instant tea, unsweetened
1 cup white grape juice
1 gallon water

Mix all ingredients together. Serves 20.

Sparkling Spritzer

48 ounces apple juice
24 ounces white grape juice
One 12-ounce can frozen lemonade, thawed
34 ounces club soda, chilled

Mix all ingredients together and keep chilled. Serves 20.

Mocha Punch

7 cups brewed coffee, chilled
½ gallon chocolate ice cream, softened
4 cups whipped topping
¼ cup rum
Grated semi-sweet chocolate

Combine coffee, half of ice cream, and 3 cups whipped topping in a large mixing bowl; stir gently with a wire whisk until smooth. Add rum; stir gently. Add remaining ice cream. Garnish each serving with whipped topping and grated chocolate. Makes 1 gallon.

Pink Poinsettia Punch

2 quarts cranberry juice
One 12-ounce can frozen concentrated pink lemonade, thawed
3½ cups cold water
1 quart ginger ale

Mix all ingredients together. Serves 15.

Fast and Festive Fruit Punch

6 pints cranberry juice cocktail
1½ quarts orange juice
1½ cups water
2½ cups lemon juice
3 cups pineapple juice
3 cups sugar

Mix all ingredients, chill and serve. Serves 30.

Breads

Butter 'em up Biscuits

2 cups self-rising flour
4 tablespoons mayonnaise
1 cup milk
½ cup shredded cheddar cheese

Mix all ingredients together and drop by tablespoon into greased muffin cups.
Bake at 400 degrees for 12 minutes. Makes 12.

Beer Biscuits

3 cups biscuit mix
3 tablespoons sugar
One 12-ounce can beer

Mix dry ingredients first. Pour in beer and stir until blended. It does not need to be smooth. Fill greased muffin tins ½ full. Bake at 400 degrees for 15 minutes. Serves 8.

Delicious Dinner Rolls

1 package dry yeast
2 tablespoons warm water
2 cups milk
½ cup sugar
½ cup shortening
5 cups flour
¾ teaspoon salt

Dissolve yeast in warm water; let stand 5 minutes. In a saucepan cook milk, sugar, and shortening on low until shortening melts. After mixture has cooled, mix into yeast. With an electric mixer, slowly add 2½ cups flour and salt to yeast. When well blended, add remaining flour to make a soft dough. Knead dough for 8 minutes until smooth and elastic. Grease dough and place in a bowl; cover and refrigerate for at least 8 hours and up to 3 days. Remove desired amount of dough and form into 1½-inch balls and place in a greased pan. In a warm place, cover and let rise for 1 hour until doubled in bulk. Bake at 375 degrees for 20 minutes. Makes 3 dozen.

Cowboy Cornbread

1 stick butter
8 ounces sour cream
One 8-ounce can cream style corn
2 teaspoons sugar
2 eggs, beaten
1 cup self-rising cornmeal

Melt butter in iron skillet. Stir in sour cream, corn, sugar, eggs, and cornmeal.
Bake at 400 degrees for 20 to 25 minutes. Serves 6.

Poppy Cheese Bread

2½ cups biscuit mix
2 cups shredded sharp cheddar cheese
2 teaspoons poppy seeds
1 teaspoon garlic powder
2 eggs
1 cup milk
1 stick margarine, melted

Combine biscuit mix, cheese, poppy seeds, and garlic powder. Combine eggs, milk and margarine; add to biscuit mixture. Stir vigorously until well blended. Spoon into a lightly greased loaf pan and bake at 350 degrees for 35 minutes. Makes 1 loaf.

Fabulous French Bread

Two 8-ounce packages Swiss cheese slices
2 loaves French bread, sliced lengthwise
2 cups butter
2 tablespoons poppy seeds
2 tablespoons prepared mustard
¼ cup chopped onion
4 strips bacon

Place slices of Swiss cheese between sliced loaves of bread. Mix butter, poppy seeds, and mustard; cook over low heat. Sprinkle onion over bread and pour butter mixture over it. Put 2 strips bacon on top of each loaf. Wrap each loaf in foil with the seam side up. Bake at 400 degrees for 20 minutes. Broil one minute to crisp bacon. Makes 12 servings.

Honey Wheat Buns

½ cup raisins
1 cup milk, scalded
¾ cup honey
¼ cup oil
1 teaspoon salt
1 egg yolk, beaten
1 package dry yeast
1½ cups whole-wheat flour
1 cup unbleached flour
1 teaspoon ground cinnamon
¼ cup salted sunflower seeds, shelled or sunflower kernels

Soak raisins in hot water and set aside. Combine scalded milk, honey, oil, salt, and egg yolk; let cool to lukewarm temperature. Add yeast; stir until well blended. Combine flours and cinnamon; stir well. Add flour mixture to milk mixture and form a dough. Grease dough and cover in a bowl. Let rise in a warm place for 2 hours. Drain raisins and press dry. Knead sunflower seeds and raisins into dough. Form small balls and place on a greased cookie sheet. Cover and let rise in a warm place for 45 minutes. Bake at 400 degrees for eight minutes. Makes 20 buns.

Jolly Gingerbread

2¼ cups flour
¾ cup sugar
1 teaspoon baking soda
½ teaspoon baking powder
2 teaspoons ginger
1 teaspoon cinnamon
¼ teaspoon cloves
¼ teaspoon salt
¾ cup butter
¾ cup water
½ cup dark molasses

Mix flour, sugar, baking soda, baking powder, ginger, cinnamon, cloves, and salt. Add remaining ingredients; blend. Pour into a 10-inch skillet brushed with butter. Bake at 350 degrees for 40 minutes. Serves 8.

Cherry Banana Bread

½ cup dried cherries
½ cup unbleached all-purpose flour
½ teaspoon baking powder
¼ teaspoon baking soda
1 teaspoon cinnamon
¾ cup whole-wheat flour
2 tablespoons cornmeal
1 ripe banana, chopped
½ cup brown sugar
1 egg
1 tablespoon oil
¾ cup buttermilk
1 tablespoon grated orange zest

Soak cherries in warm water for 30 minutes. Sift together all-purpose flour, baking powder, baking soda, and cinnamon in a large bowl. Add whole-wheat flour and cornmeal; stir to blend. In a blender, combine banana, brown sugar, egg, oil, buttermilk, and orange zest. Stir blended ingredients into dry ingredients; gently stir until completely mixed. Drain cherries and add to batter. Spoon into a lightly greased loaf pan and bake at 350 degrees for 40 minutes. Makes 1 loaf.

Go Bananas~Nut Bread

½ cup shortening
1 cup sugar
3 well-ripened bananas, mashed
2 eggs, divided, beaten
1 tablespoon vanilla
2 cups flour
⅛ teaspoon salt
1 teaspoon baking soda
½ cup chopped pecans

Cream shortening and sugar; add bananas and eggs, one at a time. Add vanilla, dry ingredients and pecans. Bake at 350 degrees in a greased loaf pan for 45 to 50 minutes. Makes 1 loaf.

Welcome Home Sweet Bread

Three 12-ounce cans of biscuits
½ cup sugar
1½ teaspoons cinnamon
½ cup chopped pecans
1 stick margarine
½ cup brown sugar

Cut biscuits into four pieces. Put sugar, cinnamon, and pecans into a plastic bag and seal. Add biscuit pieces one at a time; shake well to coat biscuits. Drop coated biscuits into ungreased Bundt or tube pan. Boil margarine and brown sugar until sugar melts. Pour over biscuits and bake at 350 degrees for 35 minutes. Serves 10.

Zucchini Bread

3 eggs
2½ cups sugar
1 cup vegetable oil
2 cups unpeeled, shredded zucchini
3 cups self-rising flour
3 teaspoons cinnamon
1 cup chopped pecans

Beat eggs; add sugar and oil. After well blended, add remaining ingredients and bake at 325 degrees for one hour. Makes 1 loaf.

Breakfast

&

Brunch

Appetizing Applesauce Muffins

1 cup flour
1 cup oatmeal
1 teaspoon baking soda
¼ teaspoon salt
¾ teaspoon cinnamon
1 egg
½ cup honey
1 cup applesauce
2 tablespoons fresh lemon juice

Mix all ingredients together and pour into greased muffin tin. Bake at 350 degrees for 25 minutes. Serves 6.

Make Ahead Muffins

15 ounces raisin bran cereal
2½ cups sugar
5 cups flour
5 teaspoons baking soda
2 teaspoons salt
4 eggs
1 quart buttermilk
1 cup vegetable oil

Mix all ingredients in a large bowl. Store in refrigerator. Fill muffin tins ½ full. Bake at 400 degrees for 15 to 20 minutes. Mixture will keep up to 6 weeks. Serves 15.

New Year's Morning Cheese Danish

1 egg
1 teaspoon vanilla
½ cup sugar
8 ounces cream cheese
Two 10-ounce cans refrigerated crescent rolls

Separate egg. Mix egg yolk, vanilla, sugar, and cream cheese. On a greased cookie sheet, roll out 1 can of crescent rolls. Spread egg mixture on top of dough. Press out remaining can of rolls on top of mixture. Seal edges with fingertips. Whip egg white and spread on top. Bake at 350 degrees for 20 minutes. Serves 6.

Vance's Favorite Coffee Cake

1 cup margarine
2¼ cups sugar
2 eggs
1 cup sour cream
2 teaspoons vanilla
2 cups flour
1 teaspoon baking powder
1 tablespoon brown sugar
½ cup chopped pecans
½ teaspoon cinnamon
Dash of nutmeg
¼ cup powdered sugar

Cream margarine and 2 cups sugar. Add eggs, sour cream, vanilla, flour, and baking powder. In a separate bowl mix together remaining sugar, brown sugar, pecans, cinnamon and nutmeg. Pour ½ batter into a greased square pan or bundt cake pan. Sprinkle ¾ sugar-cinnamon topping mixture and cover with remaining batter. Sprinkle with remaining topping; bake at 350 degrees for 1 hour. Let cool, turn out of the pan and sprinkle with powdered sugar. Serves 12.

Coothand Coffee Cake

1 egg, beaten
8 ounces sour cream
¾ cup milk
2 packages strawberry muffin mix
½ cup powdered sugar
¼ teaspoon vanilla

Combine egg, sour cream, ½ cup milk, and muffin mix; stir just until blended. Pour into a greased 8-inch square pan or 9-inch round cake pan. Bake at 350 degrees for 35 minutes. To make a glaze, combine powdered sugar, remaining milk, and vanilla; stir until smooth. Allow cake to cool 10 minutes; remove from pan and drizzle with glaze. Serves 10.

Glazed Lemon Lassos

3 ounces cream cheese, softened
¼ cup sugar
½ teaspoon grated lemon peel
4 teaspoons lemon juice
Two 8-ounce cans refrigerated crescent rolls
½ cup powdered sugar

Combine cream cheese, sugar, lemon peel, and 2 teaspoons lemon juice; mix well and set aside. Separate crescent rolls into 8 rectangles; press perforations to seal. Spread about 2 teaspoons of cheese mixture over each rectangle. Roll dough like a jellyroll beginning at the long side. Stretch the dough and tie a loose knot. Bake at 375 degrees for 15 minutes or until golden brown. Combine powdered sugar and remaining lemon juice; drizzle over warm rolls. Serves 4.

The Best Banana Waffles

1½ cups flour
2 teaspoons baking powder
¾ teaspoon salt
1 teaspoon cinnamon
¾ teaspoon ginger
2 eggs, beaten
⅓ cup brown sugar
¾ cup milk
1 ripe banana, mashed
¼ cup molasses
¼ cup butter, melted
2 large bananas, sliced

Combine flour, baking powder, salt, cinnamon, and ginger in a bowl; mix well. Combine eggs, brown sugar, milk, mashed banana, and molasses; beat until smooth. Add egg mixture to flour; stir until moist. Add butter. Bake in a preheated lightly oiled waffle iron about 5 minutes. Serve with sliced bananas. Makes 6 waffles.

Fancy French Toast

One 29-ounce can sliced peaches
1 cup brown sugar
½ cup butter
2 tablespoons water
1 loaf French bread, sliced
5 eggs
1½ cups milk
1 tablespoon vanilla

Drain peaches and reserve syrup. In a saucepan, heat brown sugar and butter on medium heat until butter is melted. Add water and continue cooking until sauce becomes thick and foamy. Pour into 9 x 13 baking dish and cool 10 minutes. Place peaches on top of cooled sauce and cover with slices of bread placed close together. Blend together eggs, milk, and vanilla. Pour over bread, cover pan, and refrigerate overnight. Bake in 350 degree oven for 40 minutes. Loosely cover with foil for the last 10 minutes. Serve with warm reserved syrup. Makes 12 servings.

Early-Risers' Egg Tostados

½ cup chopped onion
2 tablespoons butter, melted
8 eggs, slightly beaten
8 ounces sour cream
½ cup shredded Monterey Jack cheese
2 tablespoons tomato sauce
½ teaspoon garlic salt
⅛ teaspoon black pepper
¼ teaspoon ground cumin
6 tostados
2 cups shredded lettuce
1 large tomato, chopped
1 medium green pepper, chopped
3 tablespoons chopped black olives
Salsa

Sauté onion in butter until tender. Combine eggs, ½ cup sour cream, cheese, tomato sauce, garlic salt, pepper, and cumin; mix well. Pour over onion in skillet and cook over medium heat, stirring often until eggs are firm but still moist. Set aside and keep warm. Bake tostados according to package directions. Place tostados on plates; top with lettuce, egg mixture, tomato, green pepper, remaining sour cream, and olives. Serve immediately with salsa. Serves 6.

Gritty Sausage Casserole

1½ cups quick-cooking grits
1 pound bulk sausage
½ cup chopped onion
1½ cups shredded sharp cheddar cheese
1 egg, beaten
2 tablespoons salsa

Cook grits according to package directions; set aside. Cook sausage and onion over medium heat until browned; drain. Combine grits, sausage, and remaining ingredients. In a greased baking dish, bake at 350 degrees for 30 minutes. Serves 8.

Christmas Morning Casserole

1 pound bulk sausage
½ cup chopped onion
4 eggs
2¼ cups milk
One 10¾-ounce can cream of mushroom soup
One 4-ounce can sliced mushrooms, drained
¾ teaspoon dry mustard
2¼ cups seasoned croutons
2 cups shredded cheddar cheese

Cook sausage and onion until browned; drain. Combine eggs, milk, soup, mushrooms, and mustard; mix well. Spread croutons in a lightly greased 9 x 13 baking dish and layer with sausage, then egg mixture. Cover and refrigerate overnight. Remove from refrigerator; let stand 30 minutes. Bake uncovered at 325 degrees for 50 minutes. Sprinkle cheese over the top and bake 5 minutes more. Serves 8.

High Noon Cheese~Egg Casserole

¼ cup flour
¼ teaspoon salt
¼ cup butter, melted
4 eggs
1 cup cottage cheese
½ cup chopped onion
One 4.5-ounce can green chiles
2 cups shredded Monterey Jack Cheese
One 4-ounce jar pimentos
½ cup chopped green pepper

Combine flour, salt, and butter. Add eggs, cottage cheese, onion, chiles, and cheese; mix well. Pour mixture into a lightly greased 10 x 6 baking dish. Top casserole with pimentos and green peppers. Bake uncovered at 375 degrees for 30 minutes. Serves 8.

Stampede Sausage Quiche

12 ounces bulk sausage
½ cup chopped onion
Two 9-inch pie shells, unbaked
8 ounces shredded mozzarella cheese
8 eggs, beaten
1½ cups milk
1 teaspoon salt
½ teaspoon pepper

In a skillet brown sausage and onion; drain Line pie shells with sausage mixture. Mix cheese, eggs, milk, salt, and pepper. Pour combined ingredients evenly over sausage in two pie shells. Bake at 375 degrees for 30 minutes. Serves 16.

Simple Spinach Quiche

One 10-ounce package frozen spinach
1 tablespoon vegetable oil
1 large onion, chopped
5 eggs
¼ pound Muenster cheese, shredded
½ teaspoon salt
⅛ teaspoon pepper

Thaw and drain liquid from spinach. Mix all ingredients together and place in greased 9- inch pie plate. Bake at 350 degrees for 40 minutes. Serves 6.

Rice and Sausage Supreme

2 pounds sausage
1 pound mushrooms, chopped
2 onions, chopped
¼ cup flour
½ cup evaporated milk
2½ cups chicken broth
1 teaspoon oregano
1 teaspoon salt
1 tablespoon Worcestershire sauce
1 teaspoon hot sauce
2 cups wild rice
1 cup slivered almonds, toasted

Sauté sausage; remove meat from the grease. Sauté mushrooms and onions in sausage fat; drain well. Mix flour with milk. Add broth to flour mixture and cook until thickened. Add seasonings. Mix together rice, sausage, mushrooms, and onions; pour into greased casserole dish. Pour cream mixture over rice and sprinkle with toasted almonds. Bake at 350 degrees for 30 minutes. Serves 12.

Hearty Ham Roll-Ups

One 10-ounce package frozen chopped spinach
2 cups rice, cooked
½ cup chopped onion
½ teaspoon dry mustard
2 eggs
25 slices cooked, boiled ham
One 10¾-ounce can cream of mushroom soup
½ cup sour cream
½ cup shredded cheddar cheese

Cook spinach according to package; drain and press dry. Combine spinach, rice, onion, mustard and eggs; mix well. Put 1½ tablespoons of mixture on each ham slice and roll up. Place seam down in a 9 x 13 dish. Mix soup, sour cream, and cheese; pour over roll-ups. Bake at 350 degrees for 25 minutes. Serves 15.

Soups

&

Salads

Buckin' Black Bean Soup

¼ cup olive oil
2 medium onions, chopped
4 medium cloves garlic, pressed
2 small jalapeños, minced
4 ounces chopped green chiles
1 tablespoon ground cumin
1 tablespoon chili powder
2 teaspoons salt
One 12-ounce can beer
Three 14-ounce cans black beans, drained and rinsed
2 tablespoons fresh lime juice
1 cup Monterey Jack cheese
1 cup chopped scallions

Heat oil. Add onions and sauté until soft. Stir in garlic, jalapeños, and chiles and cook for two minutes. Add seasonings and cook for one minute. Pour in beer and beans. Bring to a boil and simmer for 10 minutes. Remove 2 cups of soup from pot and puree in blender. Return to pot and add lime juice. Garnish with cheese and scallions. Serves 6.

White Christmas Chili

Three 14-ounce cans Northern beans
One 10¾-ounce can cream of chicken soup
2 medium onions, diced
2 cloves garlic, pressed
1 tablespoon oil
Three 14.5-ounce cans chicken broth
Two 4.5-ounce cans chopped green chiles
2 teaspoons cumin
1½ teaspoons dried oregano
¼ teaspoon cayenne pepper
3 cups cooked chicken, diced
1 cup shredded sharp cheddar cheese
Corn chips
Salsa
Sour cream

Place one can of beans and cream of chicken soup in the blender. Sauté onions and garlic in oil until onions are soft. Mix all ingredients except cheese, corn chips, salsa, and sour cream in a large pot. Bring to a boil then simmer for 30 minutes. This may also be cooked in a crock pot. Top with cheese, corn chips, salsa, and sour cream. Serves 12.

The Whole Enchilada Soup

1 small onion, chopped
1 clove garlic, pressed
2 tablespoons vegetable oil
One 4.5-ounce can chopped green chiles
One 14.5-ounce can beef broth
One 14.5-ounce can chicken broth
One 10¾-ounce can cream of chicken soup
One 8-ounce can white chicken chunks
1½ cups water
1 tablespoon steak sauce
2 tablespoons Worcestershire sauce
1 teaspoon ground cumin
½ teaspoon pepper
Tortilla chips
2 cups cubed processed cheese
1 cup shredded cheddar cheese
Paprika

In a large pot, sauté onion and garlic in vegetable oil. Add remaining ingredients except cheese, tortilla chips, and paprika; bring to a boil. Cover and simmer for 45 minutes. Add tortilla chips and processed cheese; cook for 10 minutes or until cheese is melted. Sprinkle with paprika and cheddar cheese. Serve with chips. Serves 8.

Texas Tortilla Soup

6 boneless chicken breasts
Six 14.5-ounce cans chicken broth
1 cup chopped green onions
1 clove garlic
2 teaspoons Worcestershire sauce
1 teaspoon chili powder
Two 14-ounce cans Mexican stewed tomatoes
½ teaspoon lemon pepper
½ teaspoon cumin
1 teaspoon pepper
One 10-ounce package corn tortillas, cut into strips
One 10¾-ounce can cream of chicken soup
1 cup shredded cheddar cheese

Cook chicken and cube. Combine first ten ingredients; bring to a boil.   Add
tortillas and simmer for 30 minutes. Add cream of chicken soup to thicken
and garnish with cheese. Serves 6.

Chop-Chop Chicken Chili

3 boneless chicken breasts, halved and diced
One 14.5-ounce can diced tomatoes with garlic and onion
1 package chili seasoning
One 10-ounce can whole kernel corn
One 14-ounce can kidney or ranch style beans, drained

Combine chicken, undrained tomatoes and seasoning mix in medium sauce pan. Cook over medium heat 5 minutes or until chicken is done. Add undrained corn and beans, simmer 5 minutes or until heated through. Serves 4.

Vintage Vegetable Soup

2 pounds beef shank
¼ cup vegetable oil
4 small leeks, chopped
2 large onions, chopped
1 green pepper, chopped
Two 16-ounce cans diced tomatoes
2 cups water
1 teaspoon salt
1 teaspoon pepper
4 celery stalks, chopped
4 carrots, chopped

Brown beef in hot oil. Add leeks, onions, green pepper, tomatoes, water, salt, and pepper; bring to a boil. Cover, reduce heat, and simmer one hour. Add celery and carrots; cover and simmer 30 minutes. Remove beef shank from soup; shred meat and add to soup. Serves 6.

Cattleman's Beef Stew

1 pound ground beef
1 cup chopped onion
1 cup chopped celery
1 tablespoon vegetable oil
One 16-ounce can diced tomatoes
2 cups water
2 cups cubed potatoes
1 cup sliced carrots
One 10-ounce package frozen vegetables, thawed and drained
1 teaspoon salt
½ teaspoon pepper

Cook beef, onion, and celery in hot oil. After beef is brown and crumbling, cover and simmer for 15 minutes; stir occasionally. Drain well. Add remaining ingredients. Bring to a boil then simmer 30 minutes. Serves 4.

Hunter's Chili

1 pound ground venison (ground beef may be substituted)
1 onion, chopped
2 packets taco seasoning
One 4.5-can chopped green chiles
Two 14.5-ounce cans Mexican-style tomatoes, diced
Two 16-ounce cans kidney beans
One 12-ounce can beer
Sour cream
Shredded mild cheddar cheese

Cook meat and onions; drain well. Place all ingredients except sour cream and cheese together in a large pot; bring to a boil. Simmer 30 minutes. Garnish with cheese and sour cream. Can be made in the crock pot. Serves 8.

Wrangler Red Mushroom Soup

1 pound fresh mushrooms, sliced
1 onion, chopped
2 cloves garlic, pressed
2 tablespoons butter
One 6-ounce can tomato paste
Three 14.5-ounce cans chicken broth
½ teaspoon pepper
Parmesan cheese

Sauté mushrooms, onion, and garlic in butter. Add remaining ingredients except Parmesan cheese and simmer 10 minutes. Sprinkle Parmesan cheese on each serving. Serves 4.

Pipin' Hot Potato Soup

16-ounce package hash brown potatoes
1 cup chopped onion
2 cups water
One 14.5-ounce can chicken broth
One 10¾-ounce can cream of celery soup
One 10¾-ounce can cream of chicken soup
2 cups milk
½ teaspoon pepper
1 teaspoon garlic salt
½ cup crumbled bacon
1 cup shredded sharp cheddar cheese
½ cup chives

In a large pot, bring hash browns, onions, water, and broth to a boil. Reduce heat and let simmer 15 minutes. Add soups, milk, and seasonings. Simmer 15 minutes then top with bacon, cheese, and chives. Serves 8.

Chicken Salad for Special Guests

½ cup butter, melted and cooled
2 cups mayonnaise
¼ cup minced parsley
½ teaspoon curry powder
¼ teaspoon pressed garlic
⅛ teaspoon marjoram
⅛ teaspoon salt
⅛ teaspoon white pepper
4 cups cooked, shredded chicken breasts
Lettuce leaves
2 cups seedless white grapes, halved
½ cup toasted slivered almonds

Combine first eight ingredients. Store in airtight container until ready to assemble. Arrange chicken on lettuce leaves; top with dressing. Garnish with grapes and almonds. This topping keeps a long time and is excellent on steamed vegetables and other foods. Serves 8.

Holiday Ham and Macaroni Salad

1½ cups corkscrew macaroni, uncooked
2 medium tomatoes, chopped and drained
1 cup frozen green peas, thawed and drained
8 ounces cooked ham, chopped
¾ cup Ranch dressing
½ cup chopped green pepper
One 4-ounce jar mushrooms, drained

Cook macaroni according to package; rinse with cold water. Combine macaroni and remaining ingredients. Cover and chill for 3 hours. Serves 6.

Broccoli Salad

1 pound sliced bacon
1 pound fresh broccoli
1 pound fresh cauliflower
1 cup shredded sharp cheddar cheese
1 cup mayonnaise
1 cup pecan halves

Cook bacon; drain and set aside. Cut up broccoli and cauliflower. Mix together broccoli, cauliflower, cheese, mayonnaise, and pecans. Add in crumbled bacon when ready to serve. Serves 8.

Potluck Pea Salad

3 eggs
Two 15-ounce cans English peas, drained
1 small purple onion, finely chopped
3 green onions, finely chopped
1 small green pepper, finely chopped
¼ cup finely chopped celery
¼ cup bread and butter pickles, finely chopped
¼ cup mayonnaise
¼ cup cubed processed cheese
1 teaspoon salt
¼ teaspoon black pepper
Paprika

Boil eggs, peel and crumble two and slice the remaining egg; set aside. Mix peas, onions, pepper, celery and pickles. Add in crumbled eggs, mayonnaise, and cheese. Season with salt and pepper. Place in serving bowl, top with sliced egg and paprika. Chill before serving. Serves 8.

Crunchy Christmas Salad

2½ cups water
One 6-ounce package lemon flavored gelatin
½ cup lemon juice
¼ teaspoon salt
1 cup diced celery
1½ cups diced Red Delicious apples
½ cup raisins
½ cup grated mild cheddar cheese

Boil 2 cups of water and mix in gelatin. Add ½ cup water, lemon juice, and salt. Chill until the consistency of an unbeaten egg white. Stir in remaining ingredients. Pour into a greased 8-inch dish. Chill for 3 hours. Serves 8.

Fruity Salad Sidekick

Two 6-ounce packages strawberry gelatin
2 cups boiling water
Two 10-ounce packages frozen strawberries
1 banana, mashed
One 20-ounce can crushed pineapple, drained
½ cup chopped pecans
1 cup sour cream

Dissolve gelatin in water; add fruits and pecans. Pour half of mixture into 8 x 8 dish. Refrigerate until congealed. Add a layer of sour cream. Pour remaining gelatin mixture and congeal. Serves 8.

Side Items

Chile Relleno Casserole

One 3-ounce can whole green chiles
6 eggs
¾ cup evaporated milk
1 teaspoon salt
½ teaspoon ground black pepper
3 cups shredded Monterey Jack cheese

Wash and seed peppers. Cut into strips. Place in greased 2-quart casserole.
Beat eggs; add milk and seasonings. Spread cheese on chiles; pour egg mixture over cheese. Bake at 350 degrees for 35 minutes. Serves 6.

Christmas Eve Casserole

1 pound shredded Monterey Jack cheese
1 pound shredded cheddar cheese
Two 4.5-ounce cans chopped green chiles
4 eggs, separated
1 tablespoon flour
⅔ cup evaporated milk
½ teaspoon salt
⅛ teaspoon pepper
Cherry tomatoes

Butter two 8 x 8 greased baking dishes. Mix cheeses and chiles together; divide evenly in dishes. Beat egg whites until stiff. Mix yolks, flour, milk, and seasonings. Fold egg whites into yolk mixture. Pour evenly over cheese in each dish. Poke with knife. Bake at 350 degrees for 30 minutes; add sliced cherry tomatoes on top. Cook for 30 more minutes. Serves 10.

Spicy Green Bean Casserole

8 ounces jalapeño cheese spread
Two 14.5-ounce cans French cut green beans
One 10¾-ounce can cream of mushroom soup
One 2.8-ounce can fried onions

Cut cheese spread into small pieces. Mix first three ingredients together.
Place in casserole dish and bake for 20 minutes at 350 degrees. When cheese
is melted, sprinkle fried onions over the top and bake for five more minutes.
Serves 6.

Pinto Beans

2 pounds pinto beans
2 white onions, chopped
½ pound salt pork, cut into pieces
½ teaspoon salt
½ teaspoon cumin
¼ teaspoon pepper

Put all ingredients in a large pot. Cover with water; bring to boil uncovered.
Cover and let simmer five hours. Serves 20.

Refried:
Brown hot bacon grease. Add 1 cup chopped onions and 1 teaspoon salt and
½ teaspoon pepper. Drain beans and mash. Stir in onions.

Barbecue Style Baked Beans

2 cups Great Northern beans
5 cups water
1 onion, chopped
1½ teaspoons salt
4 slices bacon
¼ cup molasses
4 tablespoons brown sugar
2 teaspoons dry mustard
1 cup catsup

Pour first five ingredients into pot and cook 9 to 10 hours on low. Add molasses, sugar, dry mustard and catsup to cooked beans. Serves 12.

Dirty Rice

Two 14.5-ounce cans beef broth
1 stick butter, melted
1 cup white or brown rice
One 7-ounce can sliced mushrooms

Combine all ingredients and bake covered for 1 hour at 375 degrees. Uncover and bake an additional 15 minutes or until top is golden brown. Serves 6.

Party Perfect Rice

1½ cups wild rice, cooked
1½ cups white rice, cooked
½ cup butter, melted
½ cup slivered almonds
¼ cup finely chopped celery
¼ cup chopped green pepper
¼ cup finely chopped onion
One 2-ounce jar pimentos
¼ teaspoon salt
¼ teaspoon ground black pepper

Mix all ingredients in skillet. Cover and simmer for eight minutes, stirring constantly. Serves 8.

Chow Line Rice, Corn, and Cheese Casserole

3 cups brown rice, cooked
One 10-ounce package frozen corn, thawed
1 small onion, chopped
2 cups shredded sharp cheddar cheese
1½ cups milk
½ teaspoon salt
½ teaspoon chili powder
¼ teaspoon black pepper
One 4.5-ounce can chopped green chiles
Paprika

In a large bowl combine all ingredients except the paprika; mix well. Pour into a greased 2-quart casserole dish. Sprinkle with paprika; bake at 350 degrees for 45 minutes. Serves 8.

Chile-Corn Casserole

½ cup milk
6 ounces cream cheese
24 ounces shoe peg corn, drained
2 ounces chopped green chiles
3 tablespoons butter
⅛ teaspoon black pepper
¼ teaspoon chili powder
½ cup shredded sharp cheddar cheese

In a saucepan, warm milk and cream cheese until smooth. Add corn, chiles, butter, seasonings and top with cheese. Bake at 350 degrees for 15 minutes. Serves 8.

Sweet Potato Casserole

3 cups mashed sweet potatoes
1 cup sugar
1 teaspoon vanilla
2 eggs
¼ cup milk
1 cup butter, divided
1 cup brown sugar
⅓ cup flour
1 cup chopped pecans

Mix potatoes, sugar, vanilla, eggs, milk, and ½ cup butter; pour into 1½-quart buttered casserole dish. To make topping, mix brown sugar, flour, pecans, and remaining butter; sprinkle over potato mixture. Bake at 350 degrees for 30 minutes. Serves 8.

Howdy Partner Potato Casserole

1 pound frozen hash browns, thawed
1 pint sour cream
1 packet dry onion soup mix
One 10¾-ounce can cream of chicken soup
1 cup shredded cheddar cheese
2 cups crushed potato chips

Blend all ingredients except potato chips. Bake in 9 x 12 greased baking dish for 50 minutes at 350 degrees. After removing from the oven, top with crushed potato chips. Serves 12.

Sassy Salado Spinach

Two 10-ounce packages frozen, chopped spinach
2 tablespoons chopped onion
4 tablespoons butter
2 tablespoons flour
½ cup evaporated milk
8 ounces hot jalapeño cheese spread
½ teaspoon pepper
¾ teaspoon garlic salt
1 teaspoon Worcestershire sauce
1 can fried onions

Cook spinach and reserve liquid. Sauté onion in melted butter. Add flour when onions are soft. Blend until there are no lumps. Do not overcook. Stir in the following ingredients slowly: remaining ½ cup liquid from spinach, evaporated milk, cheese until melted, seasonings and Worcestershire sauce. Add well-drained spinach immediately. Top with fried onions. Serves 6.

Cattle Drive Corn Bread Dressing

One 6-ounce package corn bread mix
1 cup chopped onion
1 cup chopped green onion
1 cup chopped celery
2 eggs
2 tablespoons butter
1 teaspoon pepper
1 teaspoon sage
Four 10¾-ounce cans chicken broth

Prepare and bake corn bread according to package directions. Crumble corn bread and mix with onions, celery, eggs, butter and seasonings. Add chicken broth to make corn bread mixture soupy. In a 9 x 13 greased baking dish, bake at 350 degrees for 25 minutes. Serves 10.

Cheese Grits

1 cup grits
4 cups water
1 stick butter
One 8-ounce roll garlic cheese
2 eggs
Milk
¼ cup shredded cheddar cheese

Cook grits in water according to package directions. Add butter and cheese to cooked grits, stirring until melted. Cool. Beat eggs and add enough milk to eggs to make 1 cup of liquid. Add egg-milk mixture to grits and pour into medium greased casserole dish. Bake at 350 degrees for 45 minutes. Sprinkle cheddar cheese on top of casserole. Serves 12.

Entrees

Border Beefy Bean Burritos

1 pound ground beef
8 flour tortillas
1 package taco seasoning
One 10¾-ounce can diced tomatoes and green chiles
One 14-ounce can refried beans
1 onion, chopped
1 cup shredded mozzarella cheese
1 cup shredded cheddar cheese
8 toothpicks
1 tomato, chopped
1 cup chopped lettuce
1 cup sour cream
1 cup salsa

Brown and drain ground beef. Warm tortillas according to package directions. Mix ground beef, taco seasoning, tomatoes and green chiles and beans together in a pot and cook until warm throughout. Spoon ¾ cup of mixture in center of the flour tortillas, sprinkle with onion and cheeses, and secure with toothpick. Place burritos in a greased 9 x 12 baking dish. Bake at 350 degrees for 10 minutes. Remove from oven and top with tomato, lettuce, sour cream, and salsa. Makes 8 burritos.

Elve's Enchilada Casserole

1 pound ground beef
1 onion, chopped
One 10¾-ounce can cream of mushroom soup
One 10¾-ounce can cream of chicken soup
One 10-ounce can enchilada sauce
One 4.5-ounce can green chiles
Tortilla chips
1 cup shredded cheddar cheese

Cook beef and drain; add onion, soups, sauce and chiles. Simmer 15 minutes. Layer tortilla chips and beef mixture. Top with cheese. Bake at 350 degrees for 10 minutes or until cheese melts. Serves 8.

Texas Homestead Hash

1 pound ground beef
1 onion, chopped
1 green pepper, chopped
Two 14.5-ounce cans diced tomatoes
1½ teaspoons chili powder
1½ teaspoons salt
1½ teaspoons pepper
1 tablespoon Worcestershire sauce
¾ cup white rice, cooked
1 cup shredded Monterey Jack cheese

Brown beef in skillet. Add onion and green pepper; cook until tender; drain fat. Add tomatoes and seasonings; bring to a boil. Stir in rice. Cover and simmer 30 minutes. Cover with Monterey Jack cheese during the last 5 minutes. Serves 6.

Rudolph's Rugged Ribeye

1 cup soy sauce
1 cup water
12 pound boneless, whole ribeye
¼ cup marjoram
¼ cup thyme
¼ cup basil
¼ cup garlic powder
⅛ cup black pepper

Mix soy sauce and water; pour over ribeye. Let marinated beef set for 30 minutes. Mix spices and rub into meat on all sides. Cook at 500 degrees for 1 hour uncovered. Reduce heat to 350 degrees for 1 hour and 15 minutes. Remove from oven and wrap in aluminum foil for 1 hour. Do not return to oven. Serves 20.

Lone Star Lasagna

1 pound ground beef
1 clove garlic, pressed
3 tablespoons parsley flakes, divided
1 teaspoon basil
3½ teaspoons salt, divided
One 1-pound can tomatoes
One 6-ounce can tomato paste
10 ounces lasagna noodles
3 cups cream-style cottage cheese
2 eggs, beaten
½ teaspoon pepper
½ cup grated Parmesan cheese
1 pound mozzarella cheese, thinly sliced

Brown meat; drain off fat. Add garlic, 1 tablespoon parsley, basil, 1½ teaspoons salt, tomatoes, and tomato paste; stir occasionally. Cook noodles. Combine cottage cheese with eggs, remaining seasonings, and Parmesan cheese. In a 13 x 9-inch baking dish, layer half the lasagna noodles, half of cottage cheese mixture, half of mozzarella cheese, and half of meat sauce. Repeat layers. Bake at 375 degrees for 30 minutes. Garnish with triangles of mozzarella cheese. Let stand 15 minutes before cutting into squares. Makes 12 servings.

Texas Branded Beef Burgundy

1½ pounds stew meat
1 package dry onion soup mix
One 10¾-ounce can cream of mushroom soup
Two 7-ounce cans mushrooms, drained
½ cup burgundy or red cooking wine

Mix all ingredients in 2-quart casserole. Cover and bake at 300 degrees for 3 hours. Stir once or twice. Serve over rice. Serves 4.

Mexican Pizza

Pizza dough
1 pound ground beef
1 packet taco seasoning
One 16-ounce can refried beans
1 cup shredded cheddar cheese
One 8-ounce jar taco sauce
One 8-ounce jar jalapeño peppers, sliced
Lettuce, shredded
Tomato, chopped

Make dough according to package directions. Brown ground beef, drain and add taco seasoning. Spread beans over dough; cover with meat. Bake at 350 degrees for 15 minutes. Cover with shredded cheese and serve with taco sauce, peppers, lettuce, and tomato on the side. Serves 4.

Big Brawl Barbecue Brisket

One 4-ounce bottle liquid smoke
One 15-ounce bottle Heinz 57
2 cups water
1½ tablespoons Worcestershire sauce
¼ teaspoon hot sauce
4 pound brisket
1½ tablespoons garlic salt
¼ cup brown sugar

Mix first five ingredients together. Sprinkle meat generously with garlic salt.
Cover meat with sauce and place in a baking pan. Cover tightly with foil.
Bake at 250 degrees for 5 hours. Uncover during the last hour. Slice meat
thinly and place in sauce. Add brown sugar. Serves 8.

Christmas Celebration Tamales

2 cups self-rising cornmeal
1½ teaspoons salt
1 teaspoon red pepper
1 teaspoon black pepper
1½ teaspoons garlic salt
2 teaspoons hot chili powder
2 teaspoons paprika
2 tablespoons cumin
1¼ cups buttermilk
⅓ cup bacon drippings
1 pound ground beef

Mix cornmeal, salt, and seasonings together. Stir in buttermilk and bacon drippings to make batter. Add beef; mix well. Place 2 tablespoons of mixed ingredients on aluminum foil. Roll 3 times. Fold ends. Boil foil wrapped tamales for 15 minutes. Serves 6.

Tasty Texican Dish

One 15-ounce can chili
¼ can water
1 cup shredded Colby cheese
1 cup shredded Monterey Jack cheese
Tortilla chips
One 8-ounce jar hot sauce

Mix chili with water. Combine cheeses. In medium baking dish layer tortilla chips, ½ cup cheese, and half of hot sauce. Pour ½ chili over layers. Start layers over again with chips, ½ cup cheese, hot sauce, and chili. Layer top with remaining cheese. Bake at 350 degrees until cheese is melted and dish is cooked through. Serves 4.

Mexican Spaghetti

1 medium onion, chopped
1 small green pepper, chopped
One 14.5-ounce can chicken broth
Two 10¾-ounce cans diced tomatoes and green chiles
One 6-ounce can tomato paste
16 ounces mild jalepeño cheese spread, cut up
12 ounces cooked spaghetti
3 cups cooked chicken

Sauté onion and pepper; stir in broth, tomatoes and green chiles and tomato paste. Bring to a boil; reduce heat, and simmer for 10 minutes. Stir in cheese; cook 1 minute or until cheese is melted. Stir in cooked pasta and chicken; cook 2 to 3 minutes or until heated through. Serves 8.

Dreamin' of a White Christmas Lasagna

8 ounces lasagna noodles
One 16-ounce jar Alfredo sauce
1 cup chicken broth
2 cups cooked chicken, cut in small pieces
1 tablespoon dried oregano
1 teaspoon garlic salt
15 ounces ricotta cheese
½ cup Parmesan cheese
1 pound mozzarella cheese
10 ounces frozen spinach, thawed and shredded
2 eggs

Cook lasagna noodles. Place Alfredo sauce, chicken broth, chicken, oregano, and garlic salt in a saucepan and simmer while cooking noodles. Combine ricotta cheese, Parmesan cheese, ½ cup of mozzarella cheese, spinach and eggs. In a 15 x 19 greased baking dish layer half lasagna noodles, half the spinach-cheese mixture, 1 cup mozzarella cheese, and 2 cups of white sauce. Repeat layers. Bake for 30 minutes at 350 degrees. Top with the remaining mozzarella cheese and cook for 15 minutes. Let stand 10 minutes. Serves 12.

Crowd Pleasin' Party Chicken

One 10¾-ounce can cream of mushroom soup
16 ounces sour cream
6 skinned, boneless chicken breasts
6 slices bacon
6 slices dried beef
Toothpicks

Mix soup and sour cream together. With a mallet, flatten chicken breast.
Wrap bacon around rolled up chicken breast; secure with a toothpick. Place
wrapped chicken breast on sliced dried beef in a lightly greased 9 x 12 baking
dish. Pour soup and sour cream mixture over the chicken and bake at 250
degrees for 3 hours. Serves 6.

Boasting Broccoli Chicken Divan

20 ounces frozen broccoli
3 cups cooked chicken, chopped
Two 10¾-ounce cans cream of chicken soup
½ cup mayonnaise
2 teaspoons lemon juice
2 cups sharp cheddar cheese
½ teaspoon black pepper
1 teaspoon garlic salt
1 teaspoon chili powder
1 cup bread crumbs

Cook broccoli and place in buttered 9 x 13 inch casserole dish. Layer chicken over broccoli. Combine soup, mayonnaise, lemon juice, cheese and seasonings; pour over the chicken. Bake at 350 degrees for 20 minutes. Top with bread crumbs and bake for 10 more minutes. Serves 12.

"Deep in the Heart" Chicken Pot Pie

One 15-ounce can assorted vegetables, drained
Two 10¾-ounce cans potato soup
¼ cup milk
2 cups diced chicken, cooked
½ teaspoon pepper
1 teaspoon salt
Two 9-inch deep-dish pie shells, unbaked

Mix and pour first six ingredients into one of the pie shells. Remove second pie shell from the aluminum bottom and use for the crust to top the pie. Bake at 350 degrees for 25 minutes. Serves 6.

Just like Grandma's Chicken and Dumplings

3 pounds boneless chicken breast
1 cup chopped celery
2½ cups flour
1 teaspoon salt
1 teaspoon pepper
2 tablespoons vegetable shortening

Cut chicken, and place in boiling water with celery. When chicken is cooked; remove from broth. Mix together 2 cups flour, salt, pepper, and shortening. Beat in 1½ cups hot chicken broth. Roll out on floured towel; cut into squares. Boil remaining broth and drop dumplings into bubbly broth. Cover and simmer for 20 minutes do not lift lid. Remove dumplings; reserve 4 cups of broth. Place dumplings on platter with chicken. To make gravy, combine cold water with remaining flour and add to 4 cups of reserved broth; stir until thick. Pour over chicken and dumplings. Serves 12.

Rice and Chicken Round-Up

4 pounds chicken breast
Two 6-ounce boxes mixed wild rice
3 onions, chopped
2 sticks butter
3 tablespoons flour
1½ cups mushroom soup
1 cup milk
Two 7-ounce cans sliced mushrooms
1 teaspoon salt
½ teaspoon pepper
1 pound sharp cheddar cheese, grated

Cook and debone chicken. Cook rice. Sauté onions in butter. Add flour, soup, milk, mushrooms, and seasonings to onions. Layer rice, chicken, and onion mixture. Add grated cheese to top. Bake at 325 degrees for 25 minutes. Serves 20.

Blazing Barbecued Chicken

½ cup butter
¼ cup lemon juice
2 tablespoons vinegar
2 tablespoons catsup
2 tablespoons salt
1½ teaspoons Worcestershire sauce
1 teaspoon hot sauce
8 chicken breasts

Mix all ingredients except chicken. Place chicken on the grill and cook for 5 minutes. Baste chicken with sauce and cook until done. Makes 8 chicken breasts.

Unbelievably Easy Chicken

3 pounds chicken pieces
1 tablespoon oil
1 cup catsup
One 12-ounce can cola

Place chicken pieces and oil in a Dutch oven. Pour catsup over meat, then pour in cola. Let simmer on top of stove with lid on for 3 hours or just before chicken is ready to come off bones. May also be prepared in a crock pot. Serves 6.

Quick Chicken Enchiladas

½ pound boneless chicken breast, cooked and shredded
1 medium onion, chopped
2 cups shredded Monterey Jack cheese
1 teaspoon salt
½ teaspoon pepper
One 10-ounce can enchilada sauce
¾ cup water
Twelve 6-inch corn tortillas

In a medium bowl, combine chicken, onion, 1 cup cheese, and seasonings. In a skillet, combine enchilada sauce and water; bring to a boil. Place tortillas in the sauce; remove when limp. Spoon ¼ cup chicken-cheese mixture into center of tortilla. Roll up tortilla and place seam down in 9 x 13 baking dish. Pour remaining sauce and cheese over the tortillas, cover the pan with foil, and bake at 350 degrees for 15 minutes. Remove foil and bake for 5 more minutes. Serves 6.

Turkey Brew Burgers

1½ pounds ground turkey
2 cups seasoned bread crumbs
1 cup beer
1 packet dry onion soup mix
1 cup shredded sharp cheddar cheese
1 egg
1 tablespoon Worcestershire sauce
1 tablespoon steak sauce

Mix all ingredients together and form large patties. Broil or grill. Makes 8 large patties.

Leftover Turkey Gumbo

1½ cups chopped green onions
1 cup chopped celery
1 cup oil
½ cup flour
4 cups chicken broth
1 pound turkey, shredded
One 14.5-ounce can diced tomatoes
One 10-ounce package cut frozen okra
1 cup white rice

Sauté onions and celery in oil. Add flour to onions and stir constantly. Add chicken broth. Stir in turkey and simmer for 3½ hours. Add tomatoes and okra and cook for 30 minutes on medium heat. Cook rice according to package directions and serve gumbo over it. Serves 4.

Desserts

Y'alls Favorite Holiday Mint Cake

1 white cake mix
5 tablespoons crème de menthe
One 16-ounce can milk chocolate frosting
One 8-ounce container whipped topping
Holiday M&Ms

Follow cake mix directions, adding 3 tablespoons of crème de menthe to the water. Bake in two round 9-inch cake pans. Let cake cool then ice with frosting. Put 2 tablespoons of crème de menthe in whipped topping and frost over the iced cake. Sprinkle top with M&Ms and refrigerate until serving. Serves 10.

Noel Swirl Cheesecake

Two 20-ounce rolls chocolate and white fudge cookie dough
16 ounces cream cheese
⅓ cup sugar
1 tablespoon vanilla

Grease 9 x 13 baking dish and press one roll of cookie dough on the bottom of the pan. Mix together cream cheese, sugar, and vanilla. Spoon mixture over cookie dough. Top with other roll of cookie dough. Cook covered at 350 degrees for 15 minutes. Uncover and cook 15 more minutes. Serves 20.

Yippee-Kay-Oreo Cheesecake

5 large eggs
Three 8-ounce packages cream cheese
4 cups crushed Oreos
5 tablespoons butter, melted
1 cup sugar

Allow eggs and cream cheese to reach room temperature. Prepare crust by mixing 2 cups of Oreo crumbs and melted butter until well blended. Press into a 9-inch springform pan. Beat together cream cheese, sugar and eggs at medium speed until smooth and fluffy. Stir in remaining Oreo crumbs. Bake cheesecake covered for 25 minutes at 300 degrees. Remove foil and cook for 25 more minutes. Turn off oven, ajar oven door and allow cake to cool in oven for 20 minutes. Remove cake from oven and place on wire rack. After cake is completely cool, cover and refrigerate for 2 hours. Uncover cheesecake and remove from pan. Serves 10.

Holiday Date Cake

2 cups sugar
½ cup butter
1 teaspoon vanilla
1 teaspoon salt
2 eggs
1 cup water
1 cup raisins
3 cups flour
1 teaspoon baking powder
1 teaspoon baking soda
1 cup chopped dates
¾ cup pecans pieces
2 cups chopped apples
1 teaspoon cinnamon

Mix sugar and butter; add vanilla, salt, and eggs. Bring water to a boil and add raisins; boil two minutes. Add raisins, flour, baking powder, baking soda and remaining ingredients. Pour in a lightly greased Bundt pan and bake at 350 degrees for 50 minutes. Serves 16.

Alamo Apple Cake

2 cups sugar
1½ cups oil
2 eggs
3 cups flour
1½ teaspoons baking soda
1 teaspoon salt
3 cups peeled, grated apples
2 cups chopped pecans
8 ounces cream cheese
½ stick butter
1 teaspoon vanilla
1 pound powdered sugar
4 tablespoons milk

Combine the sugar, oil and eggs; mix well. Sift flour with baking soda and salt; stir in sugar mixture. Add apples and 1 cup pecans; beat well. Pour into three greased and floured 9 inch cake pans or a 13 x 9 pan. Bake at 350 degrees for 35 minutes. Let cake cool and then ice. To make icing, blend cream cheese and butter well. Add vanilla. Alternate adding powdered sugar and milk; stir in remaining pecans. Spread on cake. Serves 20.

Cowboy Cut Cream Cheese Pound Cake

8 ounces cream cheese
3 sticks butter
3 cups sugar
3 cups sifted flour
⅛ teaspoon salt
6 eggs
2 tablespoons vanilla

Cream cheese, butter, and sugar. Alternate adding flour, salt and eggs, adding eggs one at a time. Mix well after each addition. Add vanilla and pour mixture in a well-greased tube pan. Bake at 350 degrees for 1 hour and 15 minutes. Serves 20.

Oil Boomin' Bundt Cake

1 box Devil's Food cake mix
One 3¾-ounce package chocolate instant pudding mix
4 eggs
½ cup cooking oil
½ cup water
1 cup sour cream
1½ cups chocolate chips
Jar Chocolate Sauce (see Gift Giving Goodies)

Mix all ingredients together except Chocolate Sauce. Bake in Bundt pan at 325 degrees for 1 hour. Warm Chocolate Sauce and drizzle over cooled cake before serving. Serves 12.

Holiday Gathering Pecan Pie Cake

1 box yellow cake mix
1 cup brown sugar
2 sticks butter, melted
4 eggs
2 tablespoons water
2 cups chopped pecans
1 cup sugar
1 cup light corn syrup
1 cup milk
1 tablespoon vanilla

Mix together ⅓ cake mix, brown sugar, 1 stick of butter, 2 eggs, water, and pecans. Spread into a greased 9 x 13 glass pan and bake at 325 degrees for 20 minutes. While baking, mix together sugar, syrup, 2 eggs, remaining butter and cake mix, milk and vanilla. Blend with an electric mixer. Pour mixture over baked layer and return to the oven for 35 minutes. Cool completely before serving. Serves 20.

Stocking Stuffer Candy Cake

8 regular-sized Milky Way bars
2½ sticks margarine
4½ cups sugar
4 eggs, beaten
1¼ cups buttermilk
3 cups flour
½ teaspoon baking soda
1 teaspoon vanilla
1 cup chopped pecans
1 cup sweetened condensed milk
1 cup marshmallow cream
6 ounces chocolate chips

Melt candy bars with 1 stick of margarine; let cool. Cream together 2 cups sugar, ½ stick margarine, and eggs; add buttermilk. Beat in flour, baking soda, vanilla, and pecans. Mix with Milky Way mixture. Bake at 350 degrees for 1 hour and 20 minutes. Let cool one hour in the pan and then remove from pan; let cool completely on wire rack.

To prepare icing, cook remaining sugar, milk and margarine until it reaches soft ball stage. Remove from heat; add marshmallow cream and chocolate chips. Spread onto cake. Makes a sheet cake or 10-inch tube pan. Serves 20.

Mrs. Claus's Chocolate Pecan Pie

1 cup sugar
½ cup flour
¼ pound butter, melted
3 eggs
1 teaspoon vanilla
4 ounces semi-sweet chocolate chips
4 ounces vanilla chips
1 cup chopped pecans
1 tablespoon bourbon
One 9-inch pie shell, unbaked

Mix together sugar, flour and butter. Beat in eggs. Add vanilla, chips, pecans, bourbon and mix. Pour into pie shell and bake for 30 minutes at 350 degrees. Serves 8.

Velma's Prized Pecan Pie

1 stick butter
1 cup light corn syrup
½ cup sugar
3 eggs
⅛ teaspoon salt
1 teaspoon vanilla
1 cup pecans
One 9-inch pie shell, unbaked

Cook butter until lightly brown. Add syrup; continue cooking. Mix in sugar and cook one minute until thick. Let syrup mixture cool. Beat eggs with salt and vanilla. Pour syrup mixture over eggs and beat. Put pecans in bottom of pie shell. Pour pie mixture over pecans. Bake at 350 degrees for 10 minutes, then turn oven down to 250 degrees and cook for 20 more minutes. Serves 8.

Big Ol' Brownie Pie

1 cup sugar
2 eggs, beaten
1 tablespoon vanilla
1 stick butter, melted
¼ cup cocoa
¼ cup flour
One 9-inch pie shell, unbaked

Mix together first six ingredients and place in pie shell. Bake at 350 degrees for 20 to 25 minutes. Serves 6.

Prairie Peanut Pie

2½ cups sugar
1 cup boiling water
2 tablespoons flour
5 eggs, separated
2 cups milk
1 cup chopped peanuts
1 teaspoon vanilla
Two 9-inch pie shells, prebaked

Place 1 cup sugar in skillet; cook over medium heat, stirring constantly until sugar melts and forms a light brown sugar. Reduce heat to low; gradually add boiling water, stirring constantly. Remove from heat. Combine 1 cup sugar and flour in a saucepan; stir well. Add egg yolks, milk and caramelized sugar mixture. Cook over low heat, stirring constantly until mixture thickens. Stir chopped peanuts and vanilla into mixture. Pour into pie shells. At room-temperature, beat egg whites until foamy. Gradually add ½ cup sugar, 1 tablespoon at a time, beating until stiff peaks form. Spread meringue over hot filling. Bake at 350 degrees for 15 minutes until golden brown. Let pies cool to room temperature. Makes 2 pies.

Circle P Pumpkin Pie

3 eggs
1 cup canned pumpkin, mashed
½ cup brown sugar
1 teaspoon vanilla
1 cup half-and-half
¼ teaspoon salt
½ teaspoon ground cinnamon
¼ teaspoon ground mace
¼ teaspoon ground cloves
One 9-inch pie shell, unbaked
2 tablespoons candied, finely chopped ginger

Beat eggs and combine with next 8 ingredients. Pour into pie shell and sprinkle with candied ginger. Bake at 375 degrees for 30 minutes. Serves 8.

Boot Scootin' Sour Cream Pie

2 eggs
1½ cups sour cream
1 cup sugar
2 tablespoons flour
1 teaspoon vanilla
½ cup raisins
½ cup pecans
One 9-inch pie shell, unbaked

With an electric mixer, beat eggs, sour cream, sugar, flour, and vanilla at medium speed until well-blended. Stir in raisins and pecans. Pour mixture into pie shell. Bake at 400 degrees for 10 minutes; reduce heat to 350 degrees and bake 30 more minutes or until pie is set. Serves 8.

Longhorn Layer Delight

1 stick margarine, softened
1 cup flour
¾ cup chopped pecans
8 ounces cream cheese
8 ounces whipped topping
1 cup powdered sugar
1¼ cups coconut
2 cups milk
One 3¾-ounce box instant vanilla pie filling

Blend margarine, flour, and ½ cup pecans with an electric mixer at medium speed. Place in the bottom of a 9 x 13 baking dish. Bake at 350 degrees for 20 minutes. Mix cream cheese, 1 cup whipped topping, powdered sugar, and 1 cup coconut together and spread over bottom crust. In a saucepan, cook milk and pie filling together; cool and pour over cream cheese mixture. Spread remainder of whipped topping over the pie filling mixture. Toast remaining coconut and pecans and sprinkle on top of whipped topping. Serves 20.

Snow-Capped Brownies

1 box Devil's Food cake mix
5 ounces sweetened condensed milk
16 ounces caramels
2 cups white chocolate chips

Make cake batter according to directions. Pour half of the cake mix in a 9 x 13 cake pan and bake for 10 minutes. In a saucepan, melt caramels on low with sweetened milk; stir constantly. Layer caramel mixture, 1 cup white chocolate chips, and remaining cake batter. Bake at 350 degrees for 20 minutes. After cake cools completely, sprinkle with remaining chips. Serves 20.

Texas Million Mint Brownies

1 cup sugar
1¾ cups butter, divided
4 eggs, beaten
1 cup flour
16 ounces chocolate syrup
1 teaspoon vanilla
½ teaspoon peppermint extract
2 tablespoons milk
2 cups powdered sugar
6 drops green food coloring
1 cup chocolate chips

Blend sugar, ½ cup butter and eggs. Mix in flour, syrup, and vanilla. Pour into 9 x 13 greased pan. Bake at 350 degrees for 25 minutes. Prepare frosting by mixing peppermint, milk, powdered sugar, ½ cup butter, and food coloring. Mix ingredients until smooth. Spread over cooled cake. Melt remaining butter and chocolate chips over medium heat. Drizzle over frosting. Serves 20.

Cowhand Cranberry Cobbler

3 cups cranberries, rinsed and drained
¾ cup chopped walnuts
¾ cup sugar
1 egg
½ cup flour
⅓ cup butter, melted

Mix cranberries, walnuts, and sugar together and place in a lightly greased 8-inch square baking dish. With an electric mixer, beat egg at high speed until smooth and slightly thickened. Add flour and butter; beat at low speed until smooth. Spoon batter over berry mixture; bake at 325 degrees for 50 minutes or until lightly browned. Serves 6.

Ropin' Rich Chocolate Trifle

9 x 13 pan of brownies
One 3¾-ounce package instant chocolate pudding
1½ cups chocolate milk
Two 12-ounce containers whipped topping
⅔ cup chocolate syrup
2 milk chocolate candy bars, broken

Break brownies into small pieces. Mix pudding with milk and 1 cup of whipped topping. Layer: brownies, syrup, candy bar pieces, pudding, and whipped topping. Repeat layers. Refrigerate for two hours. Serves 12.

Candies

&

Cookies

Beloved Bonbons

1 can sweetened condensed milk
2 pounds powdered sugar
2 ounces coconut
2 sticks butter, softened
2 teaspoons vanilla
12 ounces chopped pecans
1 pound chocolate almond bark

Combine all ingredients except for chocolate almond bark. Knead with hands. Refrigerate until cold and form into balls. Melt chocolate on low. Use toothpicks to dip balls into chocolate. Place on wax paper and refrigerate until set. Makes 5 dozen.

Bluebonnet Buttermilk Fudge

3 cups sugar
3 tablespoons vinegar
1½ cups buttermilk
¼ teaspoon baking soda
½ stick margarine

Bring sugar, vinegar, and buttermilk to a boil; add baking soda. Cook until soft-ball stage. Remove from heat; add margarine. Beat until cool and pour into a greased 9 x 11 baking dish. Makes 3 dozen.

Texas Tea Cakes

1 cup butter, softened
2¼ cups sugar
4 eggs
4½ cups flour
1 teaspoon baking powder
1 teaspoon baking soda
½ teaspoon nutmeg
¼ cup buttermilk
1 teaspoon vanilla

Mix butter and sugar with an electric mixer. Add eggs and continue to beat well. Combine flour, baking powder, baking soda, and nutmeg; add to butter mixture. Add buttermilk and vanilla; beat until smooth. Drop by tablespoons onto greased cookie sheet. Bake at 375 degrees for 8 minutes. Makes 6 dozen.

Santa's Helpers Cookies

½ cup sugar
½ cup brown sugar
1 cup flour
½ teaspoon salt
½ teaspoon baking powder
½ teaspoon baking soda
1 cup corn flakes
½ cup coconut
¾ cup chocolate chips
1 cup oats
1 stick butter, melted
1 egg
1 teaspoon vanilla

Mix first 10 ingredients together. Add butter, egg, and vanilla. Stir well.
Bake at 350 degrees for 10 minutes. Makes 3 dozen cookies.

Darlin' Dinner Mint Cookies

2 egg whites
⅔ cup sugar
¼ teaspoon salt
⅛ teaspoon peppermint extract
1½ cups chocolate chips
Green food coloring

Heat oven to 375 degrees. Slowly beat egg whites adding sugar gradually.
When stiff, add salt and peppermint. Fold in chocolate chips; add food coloring. Drop on foil lined cookie sheet and place in oven. Turn off oven and do not open oven door for 3 hours or overnight. Makes 36 cookies.

Mexican Wedding Cookies

½ pound margarine
5 tablespoons sugar
2 teaspoons vanilla
2 cups flour
2 cups pecan pieces
Powdered sugar

Blend margarine and sugar; add vanilla. Mix flour and pecans; add to margarine mixture. Knead mixture; roll into small balls and pat flat. Bake on ungreased cookie sheet at 325 degrees for 15 minutes. Roll in powdered sugar. Makes 4 dozen cookies.

Howdy Dolly Cookies

1 stick margarine
2 cups vanilla wafer crumbs
1 cup chocolate chips
1 cup coconut
½ cup chopped pecans
One 10-ounce can sweetened condensed milk

Melt margarine in 9 x 13 glass pan. Sprinkle wafer crumbs over margarine and pat down to make a crust. Layer chocolate chips, coconut, and pecans; press down each layer. Cover entire surface with sweetened milk. Bake at 350 degrees for 30 minutes. Let set 5 minutes. Makes 24 bars.

Christmas M & M Chocolate Chip Cookies

3 sticks margarine, softened
1 stick butter, softened
1½ cups sugar
1½ cups brown sugar
4 eggs
1 tablespoon Mexican vanilla
6 cups flour
2 teaspoons salt
2 teaspoons baking soda
1 teaspoon cinnamon
2 cups chocolate chips
2 cups Holiday M&Ms

With an electric mixer, beat margarine and butter together very well. Add sugar, brown sugar, eggs, and vanilla; continue to beat. Fold in flour, salt, baking soda, and cinnamon; mix well. Add chocolate chips and M&Ms. Place generous scoops on greased cookie sheet. Bake at 350 degrees for 10 minutes. Makes 4 dozen.

Coconut Cornflake Squares

1½ cups sugar
¾ cup light corn syrup
1½ cups peanut butter
6 cups cornflakes
½ cup coconut

Mix sugar and syrup; cook for 2 minutes. Add remaining ingredients. Pour onto greased cookie sheet; let cool and cut into squares. Makes 4 dozen.

Prairie Pralines

1 package butterscotch pudding
1 cup white sugar
½ cup brown sugar
½ cup evaporated milk
1 tablespoon butter
1½ cups chopped pecans

Mix first five ingredients; cook and stir over low heat until sugar dissolves. Add pecans; boil 2 to 5 minutes or until soft-ball stage. Beat until shiny; drop by spoonfuls on wax paper to cool. Makes 2 dozen.

Trail Dust Turtles

3 tablespoons butter
30 Kraft caramels, unwrapped
1 cup chopped pecans
2 cups chocolate chips

Melt butter; add caramels and melt to liquid form. Add pecans and stir until well blended. Drop by teaspoons onto a greased pan. Melt chocolate chips over low heat and dip caramel-pecans into mixture. After coated with chocolate place them in the refrigerator on waxed paper until they are set. Makes 2 dozen.

Giddyap Goo Goo Clusters

2 pounds chocolate bark
1 cup crunchy peanut butter
2 cups Rice Krispies cereal
2 cups peanuts
2 cups miniature marshmallows

Place bark in a greased pan. Melt over low heat for 10 minutes. When melted, add next three ingredients and stir. Add marshmallows last. When all ingredients are well melted, spoon on wax paper and allow to set. Makes 4 dozen.

Butter Pecan Graham Snacks

½ cup butter
½ cup margarine
½ cup sugar
1 cup chopped pecans
1½ packages graham crackers

Mix butter, margarine, and sugar together; boil 2 minutes, stirring constantly. Mix in pecans. Pour over graham crackers placed on a cookie sheet. Bake at 350 degrees for 8 minutes. Let sit 2 minutes and cut on cookie sheet while still warm. Let cool completely on cookie sheet; remove and keep in airtight container. Serves 20.

Laredo Lemon Squares

2½ cups flour, divided
½ cup powdered sugar
1 cup butter, melted
4 eggs, beaten
2 cups sugar
½ cup lemon juice
½ teaspoon baking powder

Sift together 2 cups flour and powdered sugar. Mix in butter and stir until crumbly. Press into a 13 x 9 pan. Bake at 350 degrees for 20 minutes. Beat eggs, sugar, and lemon juice. Sift in ½ cup flour and baking powder. Pour over crust. Bake at 350 degrees for 25 more minutes. Sprinkle with additional powdered sugar. Cool slightly and cut. Makes 2 dozen.

Gift Giving Goodies

Popular Peanut Butter Balls

1 cup peanut butter
1½ cups sugar
3¾ cups powdered sugar
2 sticks butter, melted
1 cup graham cracker crumbs
2 cups chocolate chips, melted
1 tablespoon vegetable shortening

Mix first five ingredients together with an electric mixer. Roll peanut butter mixture into quarter-size balls; let set for 10 minutes until hardened. Melt chocolate and shortening over low heat; stir constantly until chocolate is melted. Use a toothpick to dip balls in chocolate. Chill in the refrigerator until chocolate is set. Makes 5 dozen balls.

Borderline Brandy Balls

1¼ cups butter, softened
½ cup sugar
1 egg yolk
3 cups flour
¼ teaspoon salt
¼ cup brandy
1 cup chopped pecans
1 cup powdered sugar

Cream butter and sugar; add egg yolk and mix well. Combine flour and salt. Gradually add flour mixture to butter mixture alternating with brandy. Stir in pecans. Chill dough 1 hour. Roll into balls on a greased cookie sheet. Bake at 350 degrees for 10 minutes. Let cool slightly and roll in powdered sugar. Makes 5 dozen.

Martha's Toffee Candy

One 12-ounce package milk chocolate chips
2 cups roasted almonds, sliced
2 sticks butter
1 cup sugar
3 tablespoons water

Put half of chips and almonds in a buttered 9 x 12 pan. Cook butter, sugar, and water to hard crack stage. Pour over chips and almonds. Add remaining half of chips and almonds, smoothing out chocolate chips. Let harden and break into pieces. Makes a great gift in a Christmas tin.

Special Christmas Brittle

1 cup light corn syrup
1 cup sugar
1 cup water
1 teaspoon salt
1 tablespoon butter
1 pound peanuts, shelled
1 teaspoon baking soda

In a large saucepan, combine syrup, sugar, water and salt. Cook until it reaches the soft-ball stage; add butter and peanuts. Cook until brown; take candy off stove and stir in baking soda. Pour on a buttered sheet and let harden. Break into chunks. Makes a great gift in a Christmas tin.

Kid's Favorite Caramel Popcorn

4 quarts popcorn, popped
2 sticks butter
2 cups packed brown sugar
½ cup light syrup
1 teaspoon salt
½ teaspoon baking soda

Place popcorn in a large roasting pan and warm at 200 degrees. In a saucepan, combine butter, sugar, syrup, and salt; bring to a boil. Boil for 5 minutes from beginning of boil. Add baking soda; stir well. Pour over popcorn and bake 45 minutes, stirring every 15 minutes. Makes 4 quarts.

Mexicali Snack Mix

1½ cups roasted salted peanuts
1½ cups bite-sized crispy wheat square cereal
1 cup salted sunflower kernels
1 cup Cornuts
¼ cup butter, melted
2 teaspoons chili powder
¼ teaspoon ground cumin
¼ teaspoon red pepper
⅛ teaspoon garlic powder

Combine first 4 ingredients in a 15 x 10 pan; stir well. Drizzle butter over mixture and stir. Add seasonings; stir to coat well. Bake at 350 degrees for 20 minutes stirring after 10 minutes. Makes 5 cups.

Bluebonnet State's Sweet Pecans

1½ cups sugar
½ cup water
¼ cup honey
¼ teaspoon salt
½ teaspoon vanilla
3 cups pecan halves

Combine first 4 ingredients in a saucepan; mix well and cook over medium heat. After sugar dissolves, continue cooking until mixture reaches soft ball stage. Remove from heat; stir in vanilla. Beat with a wooden spoon until mixture begins to thicken. Stir in pecan halves. Pour mixture onto waxed paper and separate pecans with a fork. Let cool. Makes 4 cups.

Christmas Pickles

One 1-quart jar dill pickles
1¼ cups sugar
2 tablespoons dried onion flakes
1 teaspoon celery seed
3 tablespoons vinegar

Drain pickles and discard liquid. Slice each pickle lengthwise into quarters. Repack pickle strips in jar, adding remaining ingredients alternately with pickles. Cover and let stand at room temperature for one day. Refrigerate, shaking jar frequently to dissolve sugar. Jar will be about ⅔ full of liquid and pickle strips will be crisp.   Makes one jar.

Cranberry Relish

½ thin-skinned orange, seeded and chopped
1½ cups fresh cranberries
1 medium apple, unpeeled and chopped
One 8-ounce can pineapple tidbits, undrained

Place orange in food processor or blender and process for 3 minutes until orange peel is finely chopped. Add remaining ingredients and process until well blended and relatively smooth. Cover and chill. Makes 2½ cups.

Green Pepper Jelly

6 large green peppers
1 jalapeño pepper
1½ cups vinegar
½ teaspoon salt
6 cups sugar
1 bottle liquid pectin
Green food coloring

Cut peppers into pieces, removing seeds. Place in blender. Add vinegar and process until liquefied. Pour into saucepan; add salt and sugar. Bring to a full boil, and boil for one minute. Remove from heat and stir in pectin. Let stand 5 minutes. Stir in several drops of green food coloring. Pour into sterilized jars and seal. Yields 4½ pints. Great served over cream cheese.

Teachers Present Pear Preserves

2 quarts hard winter pears
4 cups sugar

Peel and slice pears. Sprinkle sugar over pears and let set for 2 hours. Using a non-stick saucepan, cook rapidly; boil using little water. Simmer on medium heat stirring often. Continue cooking until pears are thick and transparent. Pour into hot sterilized jars and seal. Makes 4 to 6 pints.

Chocolate Sauce

⅓ cup sugar
¼ cup cocoa
⅓ cup water
3 tablespoons light corn syrup
1 teaspoon vanilla
½ teaspoon chocolate extract

Combine sugar, cocoa, water and corn syrup and cook over medium heat until mixture boils, stirring constantly. Boil 2 minutes, stirring constantly, until smooth and glossy. Remove from heat; stir in vanilla and chocolate extract. Serve warm or cool. Makes ⅔ cup.

Red Hot Peanut Sauce

4 small garlic cloves
1 sliced gingerroot, peeled and quartered
1 small onion, chopped
1 cup salted, dry roasted peanuts
1½ cups water
2 teaspoons cornstarch
1½ teaspoons crushed red pepper flakes
2 tablespoons brown sugar
2 teaspoons soy sauce
2 teaspoons lemon juice
¾ teaspoon coconut extract

Mince garlic and gingerroot in a food processor or blender. Add onion and peanuts, one at a time. Combine ½ cup water and cornstarch; set aside. Combine peanut mixture, 1 cup water and remaining ingredients in a saucepan; cook over medium heat for 5 minutes. Add cornstarch; stirring constantly until sauce thickens. Serve with beef, poultry, and pork. Makes 2 cups.

Tasty Texas Barbecue Sauce

1 cup prepared mustard
1 cup tomato catsup
1 cup sugar
1 cup vinegar
1 teaspoon black pepper
2 tablespoons red pepper
1 tablespoon butter

Combine all ingredients and cook until dissolved; do not boil. Makes about 4 cups.

Gift-Giving Raspberry Vinegar

1½ cups frozen red raspberries
2 cups white vinegar
1 cup dry white wine

In a saucepan bring all ingredients to a boil. Boil gently, uncovered for 3 minutes. Remove from heat and cool slightly. Pour the mixture into a hot 1-quart jar. Cover loosely with a non-metal lid. Let the jar stand until mixture cools completely. Then cover the jar tightly with the lid. Let vinegar stand in a cool, dark place for 1 week. After 1 week, line a colander with a cup-shaped coffee filter. Pour vinegar through the colander and let it drain into a bowl. Transfer the strained vinegar to a clean 1½-pint bottle or jar. Makes about 3 cups.

Southwestern Marinade

1 tablespoon cumin
1 teaspoon coriander seeds
8 dried chiles, stemmed and seeded
1 tablespoon brown sugar
1 teaspoon cinnamon
½ teaspoon garlic powder
½ teaspoon salt
¼ teaspoon black pepper
¼ teaspoon red pepper

Cook cumin and coriander seeds in a small skillet over low heat; stir constantly for 3 minutes. Combine cumin, seeds, chiles and remaining ingredients with an electric blender until mixture resembles a coarse powder. Store in an airtight container. Makes ⅔ cup.

Housewarming Horseradish Mustard

1 tablespoon cornstarch
¼ teaspoon salt
2 teaspoons dry mustard
¼ cup cider vinegar
2 teaspoons prepared horseradish
¾ cup hot water
2 teaspoons honey
1 egg yolk

Combine first 3 ingredients in small saucepan; stir in vinegar and horseradish. Slowly stir in hot water and honey. Cook over low heat, stirring constantly, until thickened and bubbly. Beat egg yolk; gradually add ¼ mixture to egg yolk. Pour egg yolk mixture into saucepan; stir constantly for 1 minute. Cover and chill 3 hours. Makes ¾ cup.

Season's Best Salsa

4 green onions, chopped
1 large tomato, chopped
½ cup tomato sauce
1 cup fresh cilantro
1 tablespoon lime juice
2¼ teaspoons olive oil
1 small jalapeño pepper, stemmed and chopped
½ teaspoon white wine vinegar
½ teaspoon garlic powder
¼ teaspoon salt
⅛ teaspoon pepper

Combine all ingredients together in a blender. Blend less for a chunkier salsa.
Makes 2½ cups.

Sugar and Spice Tea Mix

1 cup lemon flavored iced tea mix
3 tablespoons orange-flavored breakfast drink
1 tablespoon nutmeg
One 4-ounce package lemonade-flavored drink mix

Combine all ingredients in a bowl; mix well. Store mixture in an airtight container. Directions for serving: stir well before using. Place 1½ teaspoons in a cup and add ¾ cup hot water. Yields 48 servings. Makes one small jar.

Santa's Mint Cocoa Mix

10 cups nonfat dry milk powder
20 ounces sifted powdered sugar
1¾ cups unsweetened cocoa powder
1½ cups instant malted milk powder
6 ounces mint flavored non-dairy creamer

Combine nonfat dry milk powder, powdered sugar, cocoa powder, malted milk powder and creamer in a large bowl. Stir until thoroughly combined. Store cocoa in an airtight container. Directions for each: place ⅓ cup cocoa mixture in a mug and add ¾ cup boiling water. Stir to dissolve. Makes about 4 jars.

Index

Appetizers

Blazing Saddle Sausage Balls, 12
Chili Con Queso Dip, 20
Colors of Christmas Artichoke Dip, 17
Fabulous Fruit Dip, 22
Guacamole Grande, 18
Holiday Ham Rolls, 14
Never Enough Cheese Bites, 10
Pineapple Cheese Ball, 15
Popular Tortilla Pinwheels, 13
Salado Spinach/Artichoke Dip, 16
Smokies in Two-Steppin' Sauce, 9
Southwest Sausage Squares, 11
Special Occasion Spread, 21
TexMex Layered Dip, 19

Beverages

Angelic Almond Tea, 30
Buckle Down Boiled Custard, 31
Cozy Christmas Eve Cocktail, 27
Easy Apple Cider, 29
Fast and Festive Fruit Punch, 36
Front Porch Tea, 32
Home for the Holidays Hot Chocolate, 25
Hostess' Favorite Hot Buttered Rum, 26
Mocha Punch, 34
Pink Poinsettia Punch, 35
Sparkling Spritzer, 33
Warm You Up Wassail, 28

Breads

Beer Biscuits, 40
Butter'em Up Biscuits, 39
Cherry Banana Bread, 47
Cowboy Cornbread, 42
Delicious Dinner Rolls, 41
Fabulous French Bread, 44
Go Bananas-Nut Bread, 48
Honey Wheat Buns, 45
Jolly Gingerbread, 46
Poppy Cheese Bread, 43
Welcome Home Sweet Bread, 49
Zucchini Bread, 50

Breakfast and Brunch

Appetizing Applesauce Muffins, 53

Best Banana Waffles, 59
Christmas Morning Casserole, 63
Coolhand Coffee Cake, 57
Early-Risers Egg Tostados, 61
Fancy French Toast, 60
Glazed Lemon Lassos, 58
Gritty Sausage Casserole, 62
Hearty Ham Roll-Ups, 68
High Noon Cheese-Egg Casserole, 64
Make Ahead Muffins, 54
New Year's Morning Cheese Danish, 55
Rice and Sausage Supreme, 67
Simple Spinach Quiche, 66
Stampede Sausage Quiche, 65
Vance's Favorite Coffee Cake, 56

Candies and Cookies

Beloved Bonbons, 151
Bluebonnet Buttermilk Fudge, 152
Butter Pecan Graham Snacks, 163
Christmas M&M Chocolate Chip Cookies, 158
Coconut Cornflake Squares, 159
Darlin' Dinner Mint Cookies, 155
Giddyap Goo Goo Clusters, 162
Howdy Dolly Cookies, 157
Laredo Lemon Squares, 164
Mexican Wedding Cookies, 156
Prairie Pralines, 160
Santa's Helpers Cookies, 154
Texas Tea Cakes, 153
Trail Dust Turtles, 161

Desserts

Alamo Apple Cake, 133
Big Ol' Brownie Pie, 140
Boot Scootin' Sour Cream Pie, 143
Circle P Pumpkin Pie, 142
Cowboy Cut Cream Cheese Pound Cake, 134
Cowhand Cranberry Cobbler, 147
Holiday Date Cake, 132
Holiday Gathering Pecan Pie Cake, 136
Longhorn Layer Delight, 144
Mrs. Claus's Chocolate Pecan Pie, 138
Noel Swirl Cheesecake, 130
Oil Boomin' Bundt Cake, 135
Prairie Peanut Pie, 141
Ropin' Rich Chocolate Trifle, 148

Snow-Capped Brownies, 145
Stocking Stuffer Candy Cake, 137
Texas Million Mint Brownies, 146
Velma's Prized Pecan Pie, 139
Y'alls Favorite Holiday Mint Cake, 129
Yippee-Kay-Oreo Cheesecake, 131

Entrees

Big Brawl Barbecue Brisket, 112
Blazing Barbecued Chicken, 122
Boasting Broccoli Chicken Divan, 118
Border Beefy Bean Burritos, 105
Christmas Celebration Tamales, 113
Crowd Pleasin' Party Chicken, 117
"Deep in the Heart" Chicken Pot Pie, 119
Dreamin' of a White Christmas Lasagna, 116
Elve's Enchilada Casserole, 106
Just Like Grandma's Chicken and Dumplings, 120
Leftover Turkey Gumbo, 126
Lone Star Lasagna, 109
Mexican Pizza, 111
Mexican Spaghetti, 115
Quick Chicken Enchiladas, 124
Rice and Chicken Round-Up, 121
Rudolph's Rugged Ribeye, 108
Tasty Texican Dish, 114
Texas Branded Beef Burgundy, 110
Texas Homestead Hash, 107
Turkey Brew Burgers, 125
Unbelievably Easy Chicken, 123

Gifts

Bluebonnet State's Sweet Pecans, 173
Borderline Brandy Balls, 168
Chocolate Sauce, 178
Christmas Pickles, 174
Cranberry Relish, 175
Gift-Giving Raspberry Vinegar, 181
Green Pepper Jelly, 176
Housewarming Horseradish Mustard, 183
Kid's Favorite Caramel Popcorn, 171
Martha's Toffee Candy, 169
Mexicali Snack Mix, 172
Popular Peanut Butter Balls, 167
Red Hot Peanut Sauce, 179
Santa's Mint Cocoa Mix, 186
Season's Best Salsa, 184
Southwestern Marinade, 182

Special Christmas Brittle, 170
Sugar and Spice Tea Mix, 185
Tasty Texas Barbecue Sauce, 180
Teachers Present Pear Preserves, 177

Sides

Barbecue-Style Baked Beans, 93
Cattle Drive Cornbread Dressing, 101
Cheese Grits, 102
Chile-Corn Casserole, 97
Chile Relleno Casserole, 89
Chow Line Rice, Corn, and Cheese Casserole, 96
Christmas Eve Casserole, 90
Dirty Rice, 94
Howdy Partner Potato Casserole, 99
Party Perfect Rice, 95
Pinto Beans, 92
Sassy Salado Spinach, 100
Spicy Green Bean Casserole, 91
Sweet Potato Casserole, 98

Soups and Salads

Broccoli Salad, 83
Buckin' Black Bean Soup, 71
Cattleman's Beef Stew, 77
Chicken Salad for Special Guests, 81
Chop-Chop Chicken Chili, 75
Crunchy Christmas Salad, 85
Fruity Salad Sidekick, 86
Holiday Ham and Macaroni Salad, 82
Hunter's Chili, 78
Pipin' Hot Potato Soup, 80
Potluck Pea Salad, 84
Texas Tortilla Soup, 74
Vintage Vegetable Soup, 76
White Christmas Chili, 72
Whole Enchilada Soup, 73
Wrangler Red Mushroom Soup, 79

Merry Christmas from Texas

Mail to:
McClanahan Publishing House, Inc.
P.O. Box 100
Kuttawa, KY 42055

For Orders Call TOLL FREE
1-800-544-6959
Visa & MasterCard accepted

Please send me _____ copies of

Merry Christmas from Texas	@	19.95 each	_____
Postage & handling*			_____
Kentucky residents add 6% sales tax	@	1.20 each	_____

Total enclosed   _____

* Postage & handling charges - $4.00 for first book and $1.50 for each additional

Make checks or money order to McClanahan Publishing House, Inc.

Ship to:
NAME ————————————————————————————

ADDRESS ——————————————————————————

CITY——————————— STATE ————— ZIP ———————————